Next Stop

Mexico

Ginger McDonnell

Consultant

Timothy Rasinski, Ph.D.
Kent State University

Publishing Credits

Dona Herweck Rice, *Editor-in-Chief*

Robin Erickson, *Production Director*

Lee Aucoin, *Creative Director*

Conni Medina, M.A.Ed., *Editorial Director*

Jamey Acosta, *Editor*

Stephanie Reid, *Photo Editor*

Rachelle Cracchiolo, M.S.Ed., *Publisher*

Based on writing from *TIME For Kids*.

TIME For Kids and the *TIME For Kids* logo are registered trademarks of TIME Inc. Used under license.

Teacher Created Materials

5301 Oceanus Drive
Huntington Beach, CA 92649-1030
http://www.tcmpub.com

ISBN 978-1-4333-3610-2

© 2012 by Teacher Created Materials, Inc.
Printed in China
Nordica.112019.CA21901977

Table of Contents

Welcome to Mexico!

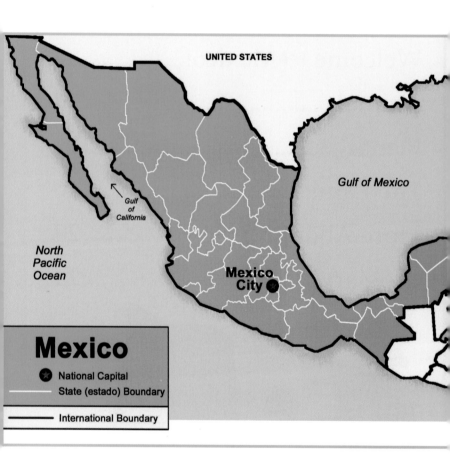

National Capital
State (estado) Boundary
International Boundary

Hola! Welcome to Mexico!

Mexico is a big country. Everywhere you go there is something new to see.

Here is a wide, blue sky over a warm, brown **desert**. A rattlesnake lies in the sun.

Here a rancher drives his **cattle** across the **plains**. They are going to the *Río Bravo,* which is a long and winding river.

U.S.A.

Río Bravo

Mexico

Along the **coast**, the mighty **ocean** roars.

In the mountain forests, a bear family searches for food.

Yes, there is something different wherever you go in Mexico.

Animals

Many animals call Mexico home. Have you ever seen a puma? You might see one in Mexico.

Coyotes also live there. You might hear a coyote howling at the moon.

Lizards, snakes, turtles, and seals are some other animals you can find there.

These are just a few of
Mexico's animals.

Plants

Many different plants live in Mexico, too. **Cactuses** grow in the deserts. Some look like people reaching to the sky.

Jungle vines and plants grow thickly in parts of Mexico. In other parts, deep forests of oak and pine trees are found.

The Land

Mexico is known for its sunny coasts. People go there to enjoy the sand and ocean waves.

Fishermen work along the coasts. They catch some of the world's best fish. Have you tried a fish taco? Tasty!

In from the coasts, mountains surround most of Mexico. Wild animals roam the forests there.

    Much of Mexico is covered
in desert plains. The land is dry,
but many plants and animals
find a way to live.

More About Mexico

Some very old buildings can be found in Mexico. There are even **pyramids** there! People come from around the world to see them.

Mexico's true name is the
United Mexican States. In
Mexico, the people say *Estados
Unidos Mexicanos*.

Mexico City is the capital of Mexico. You can find museums, universities, and tall office buildings in the city.

What else would you like to know about Mexico? This chart will tell you more important facts.

FACTS ABOUT MEXICO

Official Language:	Spanish
Leader:	president
Number of States:	31
Flag:	3 stripes (green, white, red); eagle, snake, and a cactus in the center
Independence Day:	September 16
Major Religion:	Roman Catholic
Major Crops:	corn, sugar, wheat, oranges, coffee
Money:	peso

Glossary

cactuses

cattle

coast

desert

jungle

ocean

plains

pyramid